Sandra Deneke, Inga Ettelt, Silvia Koch, Nicole Malik, Kevin Marc Patterson,
Stefanie Phlippen, Anne Sutter

Herausgeberin: Sandra Deneke

W0250995

navi

Englisch 7/8

Arbeitsheft 8

1. Auflage

Bestellnummer 61284

Bildungsverlag EINS

Haben Sie Anregungen oder Kritikpunkte zu diesem Produkt?
Dann senden Sie eine E-Mail an 61284_001@bv-1.de
Autoren und Verlag freuen sich auf Ihre Rückmeldung.

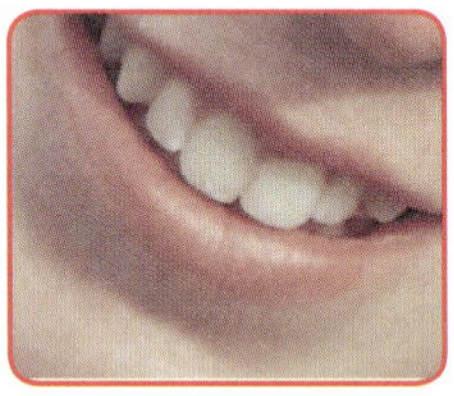

Aufgaben zur Übung der Sprechkompetenz.

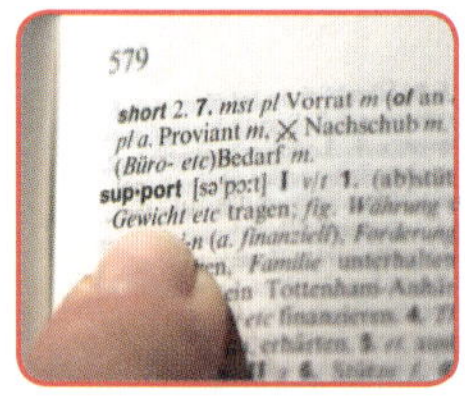

Aufgaben dienen zur Einübung des Wortschatzes.

Aufgaben zur Übung der Schreibkompetenz.

Aufgaben dienen zur Einübung bestimmter grammatikalischer Phänomene.

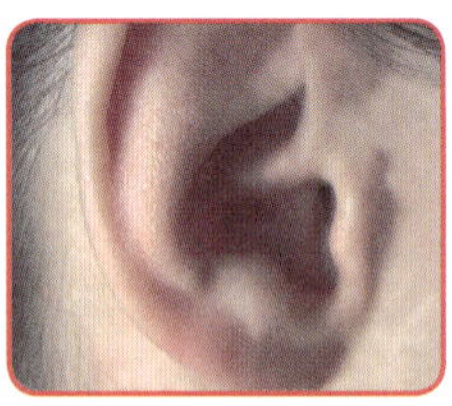

Aufgaben dienen als Hörverständnisübungen.

Dieses Symbol verweist auf weiterführende Aufgabenstellungen.

Aufgaben dienen zur Übung der Lesekompetenz.

Zu diesen Aufgaben liegt ein Text auf der zugehörigen CD vor.

Dieses Arbeitsheft deckt die Kapitel 5–9 sowie den 2. Teil von Kapitel 10 des Schülerbuchs „navi Englisch 7/8" ab. Es wird ergänzt durch das Arbeitsheft 7.

Hinweis: Die Nummerierung der Audio-Tracks basiert auf der Reihenfolge der Schülerbuchseiten und ihrer entsprechenden Arbeitsheftseiten.

www.bildungsverlag1.de

Bildungsverlag EINS GmbH
Sieglarer Straße 2, 53842 Troisdorf

ISBN 978-3-427-**61284**-1

Contents

5 My body: At the doctor's . . . 5

Section	Page	
In the waiting room	5	Bilder beschreiben
Emily is ill	6	einen längeren Erzähltext verstehen
Calling the doctor	7	nach Vorlage Dialoge schreiben
Calling the doctor	8	nach Vorlage Dialoge schreiben
Paul is ill	9	einem unbekannten Text Basisinformationen entnehmen
What can you do? What must you do?	10	ausdrücken, was man im Krankheitsfall tun kann und muss
When I've got the flu	11	ausdrücken, was man tun muss und was man nicht darf
Vocabulary: My body	12	mit dem Wörterbuch arbeiten

6 The world of work: Money and jobs . . . 13

Section	Page	
True or false or not in the text?	13	einem Text Informationen entnehmen
How much pocket money do they get?	14	einem Text Informationen entnehmen
About their pocket money	15	Notizen in einen Text übertragen
About your pocket money	16	über Taschengeld Auskunft geben
What could Emily do?	17	Vorschläge machen
You could, but would you?	18	die eigene Meinung formulieren
What would you do?	19	die eigene Meinung schriftlich formulieren
What do you think about these jobs? Would you like the job?	20	seine Meinung über Schülerjobs formulieren
Planning a flea market	21	sich über einen Flohmarktverkauf austauschen
At the flea market	22	Fragen Antworten zuordnen
At the flea market	23	ein Verkaufsgespräch verstehen
Vocabulary: The world of work	24	mit dem Wörterbuch arbeiten

7 Around the house: Energy . . . 25

Section	Page	
Things we have in the house	25	eine Liste passender Begriffe erstellen
Cut out and design your room	26	elektrische Haushaltsgeräte benennen
Why do we need electricity?	27	eine Email verfassen
How to make an electric circuit	28	eine Schaltskizze anfertigen

Contents

8 Around town: The class trip 29

Going on a class trip	29	die eigene Meinung zum Ausdruck bringen
Places to visit in London	30	Landeskunde: Sehenswürdigkeiten einer Stadt zuordnen
Paul and Emily in London	31	eine Postkarte von einer Klassenfahrt schreiben
On the tube in London	32	einen U-Bahnplan lesen und interpretieren

9 Around the world: The News 33

The daily news	33	die eigene Meinung zum Ausdruck bringen
Three tenses: simple past – simple present – will-future	34	über Gegenwärtiges, Vergangenes und Zukünftiges sprechen
Headlines	35	den Inhalt einer Schlagzeile thematisch einordnen
Today, yesterday, tomorrow	36	Aussagen über Gegenwärtiges, Vergangenes und Zukünftiges treffen

10b Around the year: Holidays 37

The first Thanksgiving	37	sich mit landeskundlichen Themen auseinandersetzen
A Thanksgiving Dinner	39	wissen, was typisch ist für ein Thanksgiving Dinner
Vocabulary: Around the year	40	mit dem Wörterbuch arbeiten

Mein Sprachenportfolio 41

Bildquellenverzeichnis

© Fotolia.com: S.14/M. (ChristianSchwier.de), 14/r. (Franz Pfluegl), 20/o. (Maria P.), 20/2. v. o. (Vasily Ryabov), 20/M. (Graça Victoria), 20/2. v. u. (Petra Gurtner), 20/u. (Fux), 29/o. l. (Lucian Binder), 29/o. r. (Increa), 29/u. l. (Sean Gladwell), 29/u. r. (schneiderpics), 30/1 (Geoffrey Métais), 30/2 (Edyta Pawlowska), 30/3 (Marko Genzel), 30/5 (Sebastian Hensel); MEV Verlags GmbH, Augsburg: S. 14/l., 30/6, 30/7, 30/8; Patterson, Kevin Marc: S. 30/4; mauritius images: Umschlagfoto; Grafiken: Pohle, Marlene

In the waiting room

1. Look at the people in the picture. What are their problems?

The old lady has got *a broken leg.*

The boy has got ______________________________.

The man has got ______________________________.

The girl has got ______________________________.

The young lady has got ______________________________.

2. Can you find the body parts in the wordsnake?

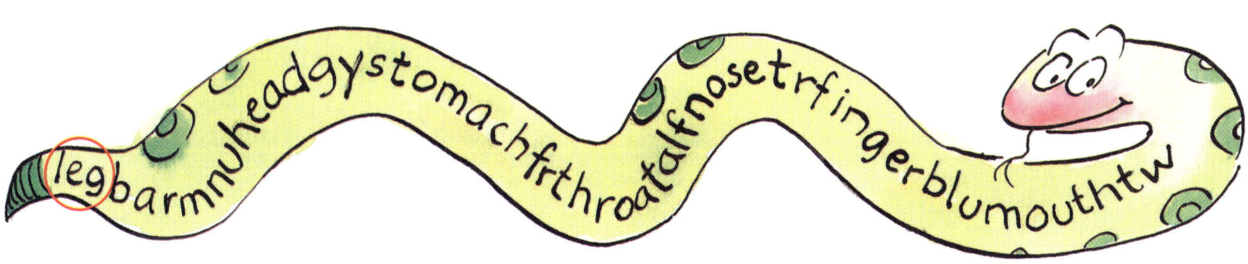

leg __________ __________ __________

__________ __________ __________ __________

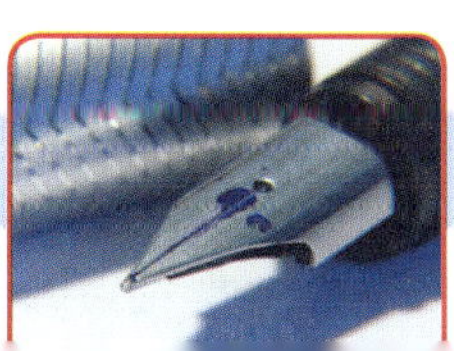

Emily is ill

Track 25

1. Listen to the text on CD.
2. Put the sentences into the correct order.

- ◯ Emily's mother takes Emily's temperature.
- ◯ She calls the doctor.
- (1) It's Monday morning.
- ◯ The receptionist says that Emily can come at 11:15.
- ◯ Emily feels very ill. She has got a sore throat.
- ◯ Emily and her mother are in the kitchen.
- ◯ Emily's mother makes breakfast.
- ◯ Her mother gives her a cup of tea with honey.
- ◯ She sends Emily back to bed.
- ◯ Then she gets the thermometer.
- ◯ It's 38.5 °C.

3. Look at these broken sentences. Connect the sentence halves and tell the story.

Emily feels	Doctor McMillan.
She has got	go to school.
Her mother gets	the thermometer.
Emily drinks	a cup of tea with honey.
Her mother sends	the doctor at 11.15.
Emily needn't	a sore throat and a cold.
But she must go to	her to bed.
Her mother calls	very ill.
Emily can come to	the doctor.

Calling the doctor

1. Read the short dialogue.

Receptionist: "Dr. McMillan's surgery. How can I help you?"

Mother: "My daughter Emily is ill.

She's got a *cold* 

and a *fever*  .

Can she come today?"

Receptionist: "Yes, she can come at *eleven fifteen* 

."

2. Finish these phone calls.

Receptionist: "Dr. McMillan's surgery. How can I help you?"

Mother: "My son Ben is ill.

He's got a ______________________  .

Can he come today?"

Receptionist: "Yes, he can come at

______________________ 

."

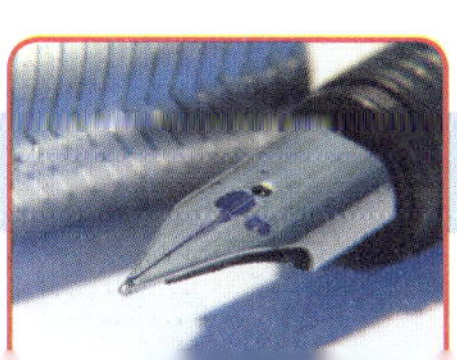

Receptionist: "Dr. McMillan's surgery. How can I help you?"

Mother: "My daughter Annie is ill.

She's got a ______________________ 

and a ______________________  .

Can she come today?"

Receptionist: "Yes, she can come at ______________________  ."

Your mother calls the doctor.

1. Draw pictures into the boxes.
2. Now find a partner and swap workbooks.
3. You write the text for your partner. Your partner writes the text for you.

Receptionist: "Dr. McMillan's surgery. How can I help you?"

Mother: "My ______________________ ______________________ is ill.

______________ 's got a [______________________]

Can ______________ come today?"

Receptionist: "Yes, ______________ can come at [______________________]."

Paul is ill

Track 27

1. Listen to the text on CD.
   Read the questions and tick the correct pictures.

When can Paul come to the doctor?

☐

☐

☐

What's his problem?

☐

☐

☐

What does the doctor do?

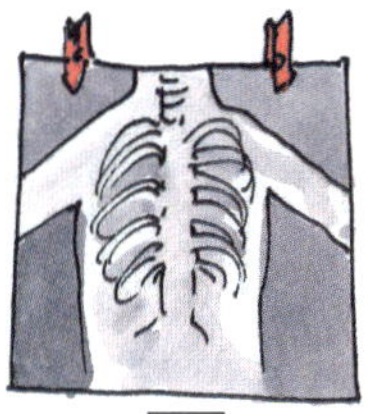
☐

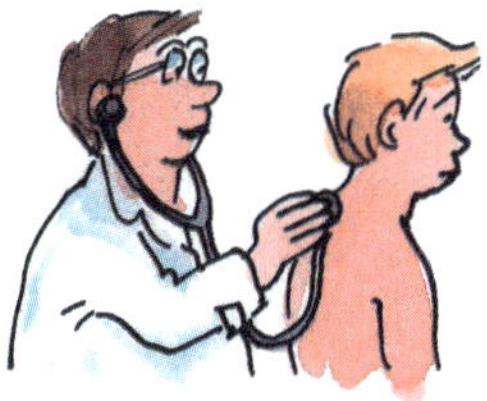
☐

☐

What's Paul's temperature?

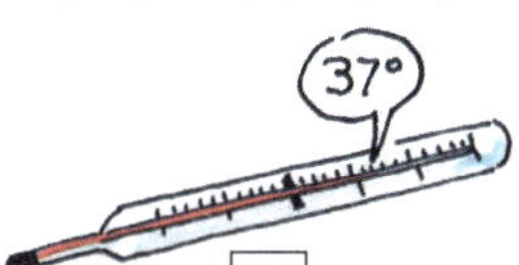

☐

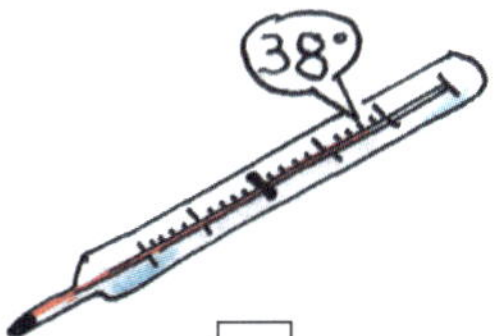

☐

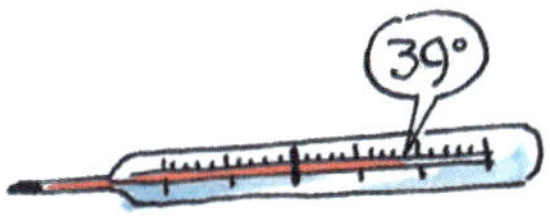

☐

What must Paul do? (Tick two pictures.)

☐

☐

☐

2. Work with a partner.
   One of you asks the question, the other one answers it.

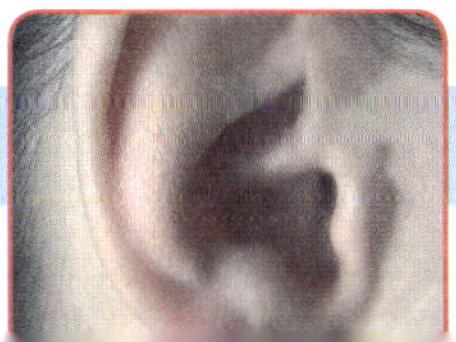

What can you do? What must you do?

1. What are these activities?
   Connect the picture and the activity.

stay in bed

go to school

write e-mails

take medicine

play football

read a book

use the computer

go shopping with my friends

listen to music

do my homework

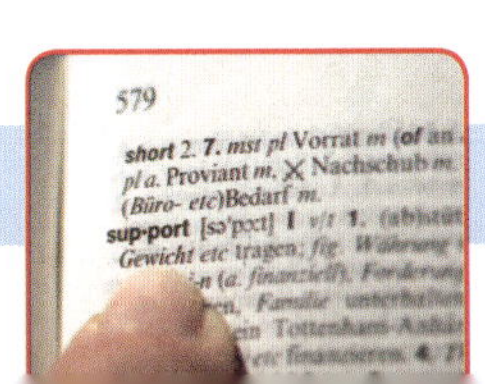

When I've got the flu

1. What about you? Can or can't you do these things?
   Use the list from the page before. You can add other activities, too.
2. Is that good or bad? Add a smiley (☺) or a grumpy (☹).

I			
can	can't	must	mustn't
		stay in bed ☺	

When I've got the flu, I can ______________________________.

I think that's ____________________.

When I've got the flu, I can't ______________________________.

I think that's ____________________.

When I've got the flu, I must ______________________________.

I think that's ____________________.

When I've got the flu, I mustn't ______________________________.

I think that's ____________________.

3. Now compare your results with a partner. What is different?
4. Collect the class results on a poster.

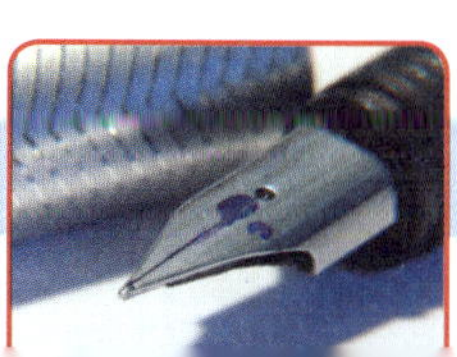

Vocabulary: My body

1. Match the pictures with the correct words. Write the number next to the word.

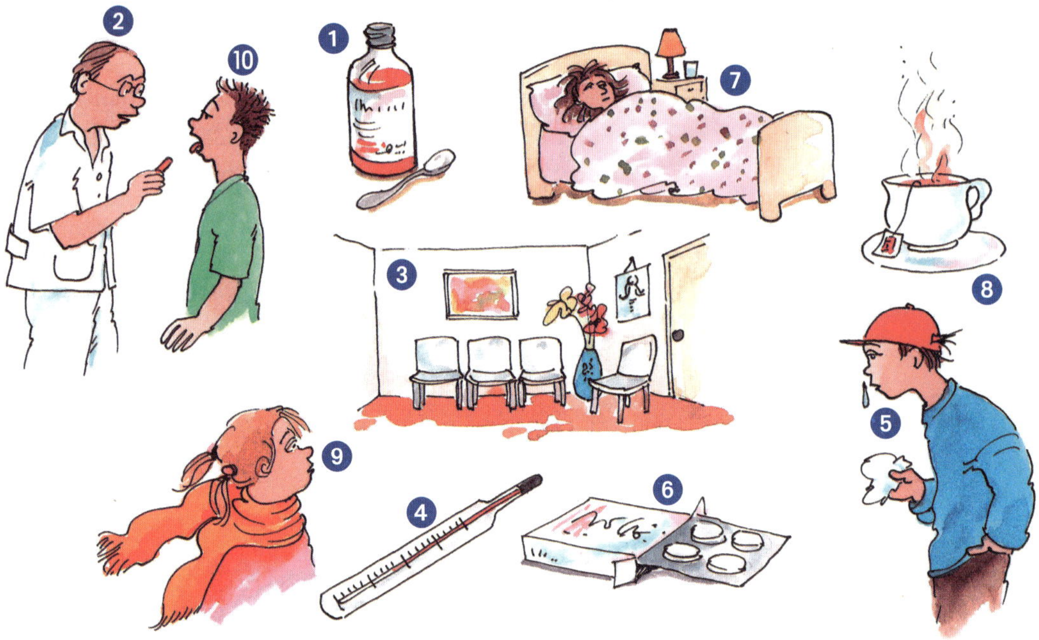

tablets

a cup of tea

a doctor

a patient

a cold

medicine

a thermometer

a waiting room

a sore throat

to stay in bed

2. Write the words into the crossword.

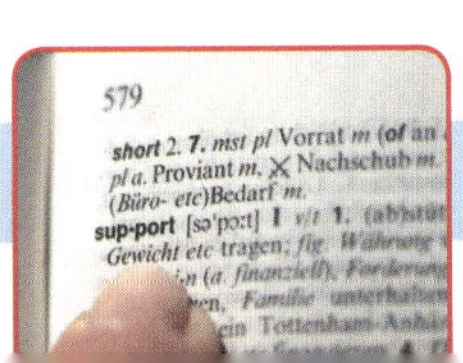

True or false or not in the text?

1. Compare the statements with the story in your textbook on pages 56 and 57. Tick the correct answers ✔.

	true	false	not in the text
It's Saturday afternoon.		✔	
Emily and Carla go window-shopping.			
Carla loves the shoes.			
The shoes are black.			
The shoes are expensive.			
Emily has enough money to buy the shoes.			
Emily has lots of shoes at home.			
Emily wants to check her piggy bank.			

	true	false	not in the text
Carla wants to buy a microwave.			
Carla wants to buy a microphone.			
Carla sings in a band.			
The microphone is cheap.			
Carla wants to take money out of her piggy bank.			
The two girls walk to school.			
It's four o'clock when Emily gets home.			
Emily has £ 9.75.			
Carla has £ 12.50.			

How much pocket money do they get?

Track 32

1. Listen to Emily, Carla, Paul and Cem. Fill in the grid.

	How much pocket money do they get?	Who gives them their pocket money?	What do they buy with their money?	Do you save up money? What for?

Emily	£ 15 per month			
Carla			– CDs	
Paul		– his father		
Cem				– new football

2. What about **you**? Fill in the grid.

You				

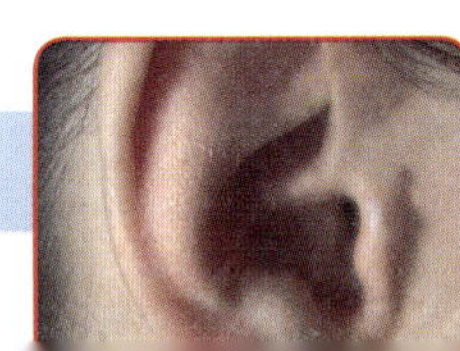

About their pocket money

1. Use the notes you took on page 14. Fill in the gaps.

Emily gets £ ____________ per ____________.

Her ____________ give her the pocket money.

Carla gets £ ____________ per ____________.

Her ____________ gives her the pocket money.

Paul gets £ ____________ per ____________.

His ____________ gives him the pocket money.

Paul gets £ ____________ per ____________.

His ____________ gives him the pocket money.

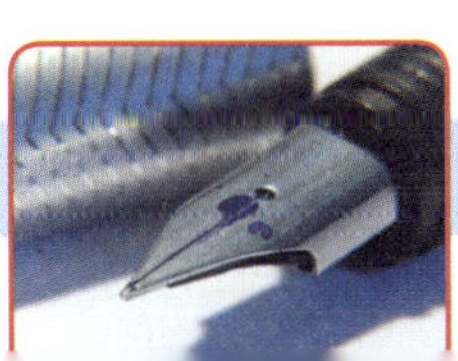

About your pocket money

1. Write about yourself.

My pocket money

My name is ____.

I'm ____________________ years old.

I get € ________________ per ____________________.

My ________________________ give/gives me

the pocket money.

With the money I buy

____

____

____

____

____

____

____

I save up money for ____________________________.

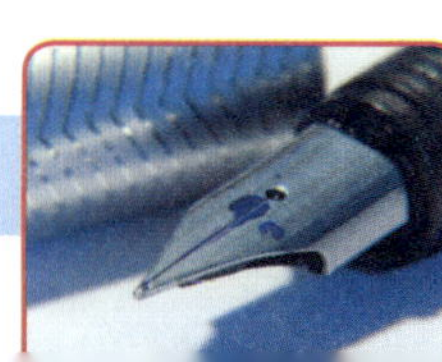

What could Emily do?

1. Look at the pictures. What could Emily do?

She could walk dogs. ______________________

____

____

____

____

2. What else could Emily do? Write down your ideas.

She could ______________________.

______________________.

______________________.

You could, but would you?

1. What kind of jobs **could** you do, but **wouldn't** you do?
   Write sentences like this:

   I could deliver newspapers, but I wouldn't.
   I don't have a bike.

I could ______________________________, but I wouldn't.

I ______________________________.

I could ______________________________, but I wouldn't.

I ______________________________.

I could ______________________________, but I wouldn't.

I ______________________________.

I could ______________________________, but I wouldn't.

I ______________________________.

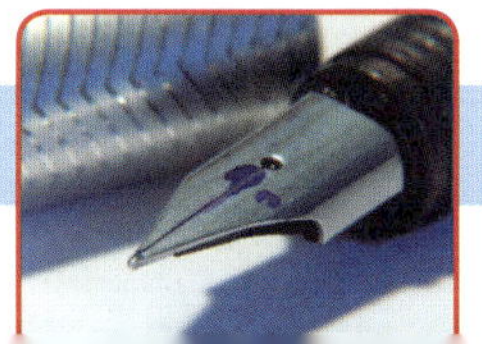

What would you do?

1. What kind of jobs would **you** do?
   Write sentences like this:

   I would clean windows. It's an easy job.

I would ____.

____.

I would ____.

____.

I would ____.

____.

I would ____.

____.

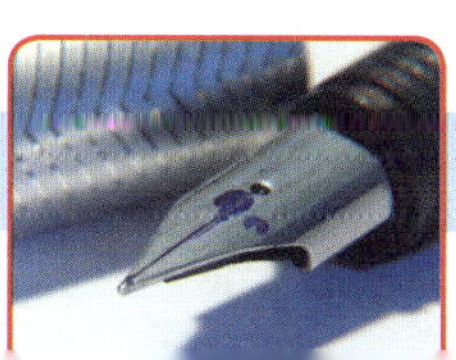

What do you think about these jobs? Would you like the job?

1. Look at these jobs. Would you like the job (pro) or wouldn't you like the job (contra)? Decide yourself and mark the faces.
2. Write down **your** arguments.

☺ ☹ *No, because I don't like cold water.*

☺ ☹ ______________________________ .

☺ ☹ ______________________________ .

☺ ☹ ______________________________ .

☺ ☹ ______________________________ .

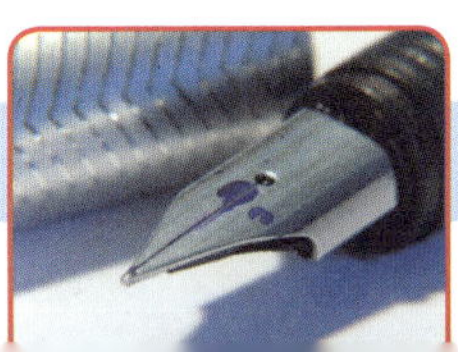

Planning a flea market

1. Imagine you are planning a flea market. What could **you** sell?
   Write sentences.

I could sell ____.

I could ____.

I ____.

____

____

2. Talk to your classmates. What could **they** sell?

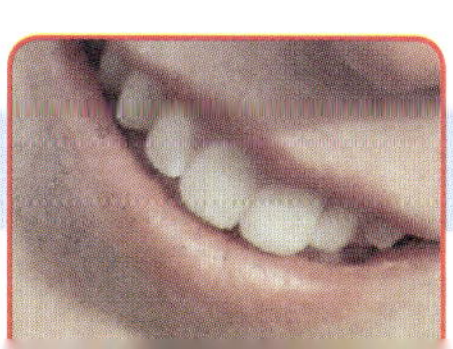

At the flea market

How much is it?

How about this DVD?

How about this beautiful vase?

How about this book?

How about this computer game?

1. Match the questions with the answers.

____

Cool, I love this film.

____

It's £ 3.

____

Yes, that's a good present for my mother. My mom loves to read.

____

It's not beautiful, it's ugly.

____

No, thank you. I don't have a computer.

At the flea market

1. Listen to the CD. Write down the information.

Track 34

What are they looking for? 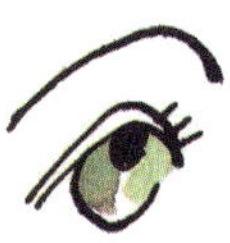		
What do they buy? 		
How much do they pay? 		

Vocabulary: The world of work

1. Match the pictures with the vocabulary. Number the sentences.

	– to help in a shop		– to work at a supermarket
1	– to baby-sit		– to paint fences
	– to walk a dog		– to repair bikes
	– to wash cars		– to do gardening
	– to deliver newspapers		– to clean windows

2. Compare with your neighbour. Write the jobs into the list.

1. *to baby-sit* ______________________ 2. ______________________

3. ______________________ 4, ______________________

5. ______________________ 6. ______________________

7. ______________________ 8. ______________________

9. ______________________ 10. ______________________

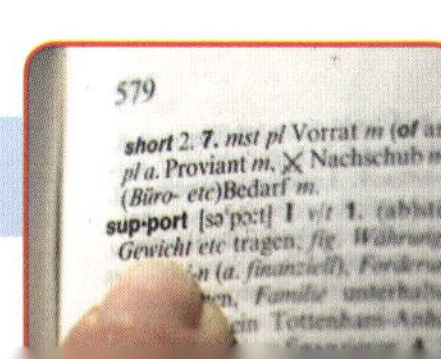

Things we have in the house

1. Look at the pictures. What have you got in your home?
   Complete the list below.

This is what we've got at home.

In our home we've got:	In our home we've **not** got:

Cut out and design your room

1. Name these objects. Write down the words.

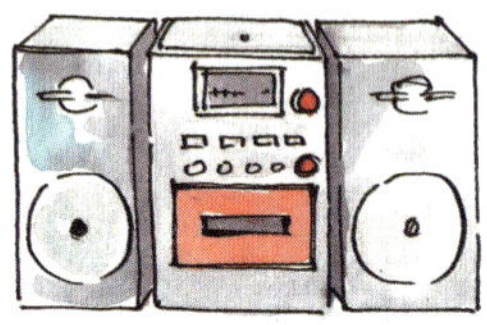

2. Cut out your “technical equipment”. You will find it on page 57.
Stick it into the plan.

3. Tell your neighbour what you really need. Choose 3 things.

What I need:	What I don’t need:

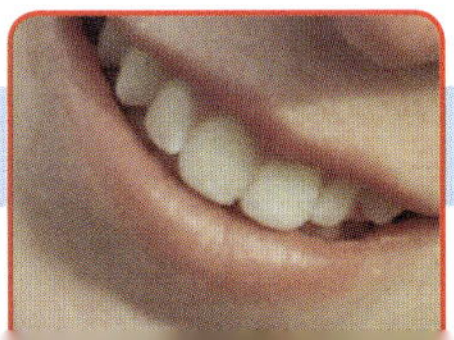

Why do we need electricity?

1. Read the text in the book on page 71 again.
   What is in the text and what is not in the text? Tick the correct sentences.

Track 39

	subject	That is …	
	We need energy …	***… true***	***… false***
1.	… because we use electricity to cook food.	✔	
2.	… because we use oil for the cars.		
3.	… because it's good for us.		
4.	… but it's also dangerous.		
5.	… and electricity doesn't create smog.		

2. Read the e-mail.

Track 40

To: Emily [emily2008@aol.com]
From: Paul [paulpaul@msn.com]
Subject: A new mp-3 player

Dear Emily,

what is your new mp-3 player like? Do you like it? How many songs can you store on it? Now my mp-3 player is broken. So I need a new one, too. Would you like to go shopping with me?

3. Answer the e-mail.

To: Paul
From: Emily
Subject: RE: A new mp-3 player

Dear Paul,

____

____

____

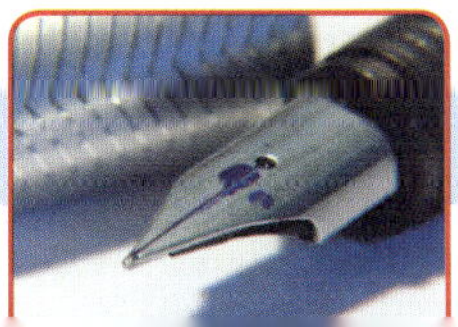

eine E-Mail verfassen

How to make an electric circuit

1. Which materials do you need to make an electric circuit? Make a list.
2. Draw an electric circuit into the box.

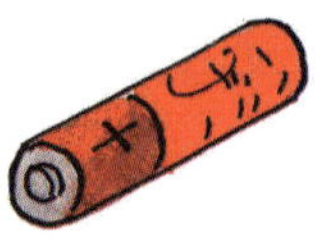

List of things for an electric circuit:

eine Schaltskizze anfertigen

Going on a class trip

1. Look at the pictures.
   Where would you like to go?
   Tick the box.

1

2

3

4

2. Choose two places and say why you would like to go there.

What's your opinion?

I would like to go to number … because...

____

____

____

____

Places to visit in London

1. Which places are in London? Circle the correct numbers.

1

2

3

4

5

8

6

7

2. Can you remember the names of these places in London?
   Do you know the other places as well?

1. ______________________________ 5. ______________________________

2. ______________________________ 6. ______________________________

3. ______________________________ 7. ______________________________

4. ______________________________ 8. ______________________________

Paul and Emily in London

1. Read the text on page 81 in the book again.
What is in the text and what is not in the text? Tick the correct sentences.

Track 47

	subject	That is …	
	Paul and Emily …	***… in the text***	***… not in the text***
1.	… are at the Tower Bridge.		✔
2.	… want to go on a boat trip on River Thames.		
3.	… are at the Houses of Parliament.		
4.	… are looking at Big Ben.		
5.	… can buy a replica of Big Ben if they want.		

2. You are on a class trip. Write a short postcard to a friend.
Tell him or her about your trip.

Dear ____________,

____

____

____

____

____

____

____

Yours ____________

To

____

____

____

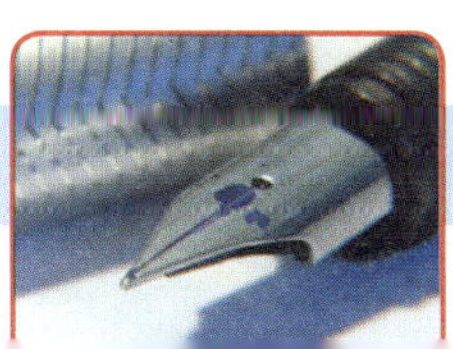

On the tube in London

1. You are at Piccadilly Circus. You want to go to another place. Name the tube lines you must take, and name the stations you pass. Look them up on page 83 in your textbook.

Track 49

Example 1:
I´m at **Piccadilly Circus**. To get to **Westminster**, I must take the **Jubilee Line**.

Example 2:
I´m at **Piccadilly Circus**. To get to **South Kensington**, I must take the **Piccadilly Line**.
I pass the stations **Hyde Park Corner** and **Knightsbridge**.

a.)
I'm at **Piccadilly Circus**. To get to ______________________________,

I must take the ______________________________.

☐ I pass the stations ______________________________.

☐ I don't pass any other stations.

b.)
I'm at **Piccadilly Circus**. To get to ______________________________,

I must take the ______________________________.

☐ I pass the stations ______________________________.

☐ I don't pass any other stations.

2. Can you get to these places if you take other lines?
Write into your exercise book.

The daily news

1. Look at the mind map.
   Which parts of the daily news do you know?
   Complete the mind map.
   weather – sports – politics – entertainment

2. Which part of the news is important to you?
   Which part is unimportant to you?

Parts of the news:

These parts are important to me:	These parts are unimportant to me:

Three tenses: simple past – simple present – will-future

1. Underline the verb in each sentence.

The Queen is in London.

There will be more sun tomorrow.

Paul McCartney arrives late to the concert.

People demonstrated yesterday.

Prime Minister says there's no need for further money.

Madonna wants another baby.

David Beckham broke his arm during a friendly match yesterday.

Beckham: "We played well yesterday."

"We can do better!"

2. Look at the sentences.
Colour sentences in the simple past **red**.
Colour sentences in the simple present **green**.
Colour sentences using the will future **blue**.

Headlines

Track 54

1. Find all the headlines which match the following themes.
   Colour political headlines yellow.
   Colour sports headlines purple.
   Colour entertainment headlines grey.
   Colour weather headlines orange.

Football star Beckham leaves Manchester United

New President in the USA

Michael Schumacher quits racing

Rihanna says music is good medicine

It will be sunny tomorrow

It will rain tomorrow

100 people killed in attack yesterday

Jack Nicholson nominated for another Oskar

2. Can you write your own headlines?
   Use newspapers to help you.

Today, yesterday, tomorrow

1. Look at the sentences. Complete them using the correct tense.

1. The sun shines *(to shine)*. **simple present**

2. Emily ________________ *(to visit)* Paul every day. **simple present**

3. Paul ________________ *(to want)* her to come every day. **simple present**

---

4. Paul ________________ *(to want)* to play football. **simple past**

5. The Prime Minister ________________ *(to arrive)* yesterday. **simple past**

6. Elton John ________________ *(to be)* happy to play the concert. **simple past**

---

7. Paul ________________ *(to arrive)* at school at nine o'clock. **will-future**

8. He ________________ *(to buy)* a newspaper today. **will-future**

9. The weather ________________ (to be) good tomorrow. **will-future**

---

10. He ________________ *(to watch)* the football match at the weekend. ***Up to you*** ☺

The first Thanksgiving

1. Cut out the pictures on page **59**.
2. Stick them in the correct order on the following pages.
3. Write down one sentence for each picture.
   If you need help, look at page **101** in the textbook.

picture 1

___

___

___

___

picture 2

___

___

___

___

picture 3

___

___

___

___

picture 4

picture 5

picture 6

picture 7

A Thanksgiving Dinner

1. What belongs to a typical Thanksgiving Dinner?
   Colour the food for a typical Thanksgiving Dinner green.

A Thanksgiving Dinner

pie

chicken

strawberry sauce

stuffed turkey

pizza

cheese

beans

ice

cranberry sauce

mashed potatoes

corn

fish

Vocabulary: Around the year

1. Match the pictures with the correct words. Use your ruler.

1

2

3

4
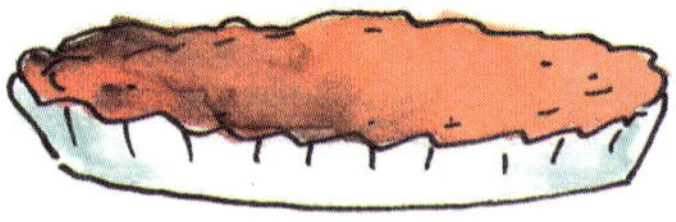

5

6

mashed potatoes

beans

corn

cranberry sauce

a stuffed turkey

a pie

2. Write down the words.

1. ______________________
2. ______________________
3. ______________________
4. ______________________
5. ______________________
6. ______________________

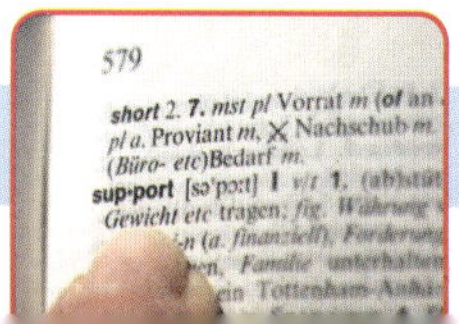

Mein Sprachenportfolio

Name: ______________________ **Datum:** ____________

Was ich schon kann

Das hat mir in Kapitel 5 “My body“ am meisten Spaß gemacht:

____

____

____

____

Das sind meine englischen Lieblingswörter und Sätze aus dem Kapitel:

____

____

____

____

____

Was ich auf Englisch sagen oder verstehen kann:

- ☐ Ich kenne die englischen Namen für verschiedene Krankheiten.
- ☐ Ich kann sagen, was mir fehlt.
- ☐ Ich kann ein Gespräch mit einem Arzt führen.
- ☐ Ich kann Anweisungen befolgen und Ratschläge geben.
- ☐ Ich kann sagen, was ich im Krankheitsfall tun kann, was ich tun muss und was ich nicht tun darf.

Vorschläge für dein Me-Book:

- Schreibe den Dialog „I feel very ill“, den du mit einem Partner geschrieben hast, noch einmal sauber ab und ergänze ihn durch passende Bilder. Hefte den Dialog in dein Me-Book ein.
- Gestalte den Text „Your mother calls the doctor“ aus deinem Arbeitsheft (S. 7) noch einmal auf einem weiteren Blatt Papier und hefte dies in dein „Me-Book“ ein.

Was ich schon kann

Das hat mir in Kapitel 6 „The world of work“ am meisten Spaß gemacht:

____

____

____

____

____

____

____

____

____

Was ich auf Englisch sagen oder verstehen kann:

- ☐ Ich kann Fragen zum Thema Taschengeld beantworten.
- ☐ Ich kann Fragen zum Thema Taschengeld stellen.
- ☐ Ich kann Freunde mit Geldproblemen beraten.
- ☐ Ich kann sagen, welche Jobs ich machen würde.
- ☐ Ich kann begründen, warum ich bestimmte Jobs machen würde oder nicht.
- ☐ Ich kann einen Flohmarkt organisieren.
- ☐ Ich kann ein Verkaufsgespräch führen.

Ein selbst geschriebener Verkaufsdialog

You: "How about ______________________________________?"

Boy: "How much is it?"

You: "That's € _______________."

Boy: "Hhhmmm… "

You: "How about this _____________________________________?"

Boy: "____."

You: "____."

Boy: "____."

You: "____."

Boy: "Well, OK, _________________________."

You: "Here you are."

Boy: "Thank you. Good bye."

Was ich schon kann

Das hat mir in Kapitel 7 „Around the house“ am meisten Spaß gemacht:

____

____

____

Was ich schon auf Englisch sagen oder verstehen kann:

- ☐ Ich kann elektrische Gegenstände benennen.
- ☐ Ich kann eine E-Mail schreiben.
- ☐ Ich kann einen elektrischen Stromkreis bauen und die Schaltskizze beschriften.

Wörter, die ich auf Englisch zu den Themen *Energie, Strom, elektrische Geräte* kenne:

Darauf achte ich, wenn ich eine E-Mail schreibe:

____

____

Was ich schon kann

Das hat mir in Kapitel 8 „Around town“ am meisten Spaß gemacht:

Das sind meine englischen Lieblingswörter und -sätze:

Was ich schon auf Englisch sagen oder verstehen kann:

- ☐ Ich kenne einige Sehenswürdigkeiten der Stadt London.
- ☐ Ich kann eine Postkarte schreiben.
- ☐ Ich kann einen U-Bahnplan lesen.
- ☐ Ich kann Bingo spielen.
- ☐ Ich kann den Inhalt des Textes „Things to know about London“ verstehen.

So arbeite ich mit dem Wörterbuch:

Name: ______________________ Datum: ____________

Was ich schon kann

Das hat mir in Kapitel 9 „Around the world" am meisten Spaß gemacht:

____

____

____

Was ich schon auf Englisch sagen oder verstehen kann:

- ☐ Ich weiß, aus welchen Bereichen eine Nachrichtensendung besteht.
- ☐ Ich kann sagen, dass etwas in der Gegenwart, in der Vergangenheit oder in der Zukunft passiert.
- ☐ Ich kann Schlagzeilen lesen, verstehen und nach Themen ordnen.

Wörter, die ich auf Englisch zu den Themen *Nachrichten* kenne:

Mind maps helfen mir bei folgenden Aufgaben:

____

____

Name: ______________________ **Datum:** ______________

Was ich schon kann

Das hat mir in Kapitel 10 „Around the world/Thanksgiving“ am meisten Spaß gemacht.

____

____

____

Was ich schon auf Englisch sagen oder verstehen kann:

- ☐ Ich kann aufzählen, was zu einem typischen Thanksgiving Dinner gehört.
- ☐ Ich kann Thanksgiving mit einem deutschen Fest vergleichen.
- ☐ Ich kann den Inhalt der Geschichte „The first Thanksgiving“ verstehen.

Wörter, die ich auf Englisch zum Thema *Thanksgiving* kenne:

7 Around the house: p. 26

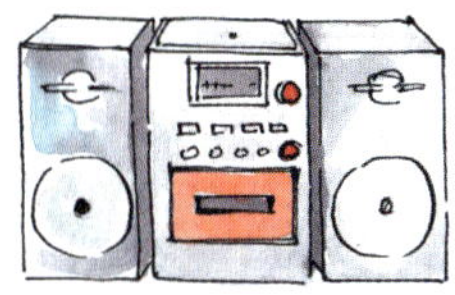

10b Around the year: p. 37, 38